Finding MINDFULNESS *in Nature*

TRIGGER™
The mental health & wellbeing publisher

ABOUT THE AUTHORS

Dr. Nina Smiley's efforts to share mindfulness with real people in real lives when they really need it began when she co-authored *The Three Minute Meditator* with her brother, David Harp, which was originally based on his master's thesis.

After earning her doctoral degree in psychology at Princeton University, Nina taught at the University of Maryland and worked for the American Psychological Association before her path led to Mohonk Mountain House in New Paltz, NY (www.mohonk.com), a unique Victorian castle resort founded in 1869, where she is now Director of Mindfulness Programming.

Nina's work in mindfulness has been seen in *O, the Oprah Magazine*, *Shape*, *Real Simple*, *Marie Claire*, and *The New York Times*. Nina leads programs and teaches private classes on mindfulness, wellness, and forest bathing. She delights in sharing simple and effective mindfulness meditation techniques that can be used anytime and anywhere.

David Harp's work as a cognitive scientist involves studying the way in which the brain obtains and processes information, then uses that information to produce our words, our actions, and our emotions.

The author of more than two dozen books, including *Mindfulness To Go: How to Meditate While You're On the Move!* and *Neural Path Therapy: How to Change Your Brain's Response to Anger, Fear, Pain, and Desire,* a corporate speaker, and a professional musician, David travels the United States and the world helping organizations work more co-operatively, more creatively, and with less stress.

His work has been featured on television and radio programs including Good Morning America and National Public Radio and can be seen at www.thethreeminutemeditator.com

Both David and Nina delight in being outdoors. They have found, along with many others, comfort and support for living in an increasingly complex world from the profound simplicity of being mindful in nature.

Finding
MINDFULNESS
in Nature

SIMPLE MEDITATION PRACTICES TO CONNECT WITH THE NATURAL WORLD

DR NINA SMILEY WITH DAVID HARP

The mental health & wellbeing publisher

Published in Great Britain 2020 by Trigger

First published as Mindfulness in Nature by Hatherleigh Press 2017

Trigger is a trading style of Shaw Callaghan Ltd & Shaw Callaghan 23 USA, INC.

The Foundation Centre

Navigation House, 48 Millgate, Newark

Nottinghamshire NG24 4TS UK

www.triggerpublishing.com

Library of Congress Cataloguing-in-Publication Data

is available upon request.

British Library Cataloguing in Publication Data

A CIP catalogue record for this book is available upon request from the British Library

ISBN: 9781789561791

This book is also available in the following eBook formats:

ePUB: 9781789561807

Cover design by stevewilliamscreative.com
Typeset by stevewilliamscreative.com

Printed and bound in Great Britain by Clays Ltd, Elcograf S.p.A.

Contents

Introduction

To seek mindfulness in nature is a meaningful part of the human experience. Delighting in the natural world, being struck by a sense of awe at the transcendent power of nature, and feeling nurtured by its depth of healing are timeless sentiments.

Mindfulness is simply a state that involves being aware of our thoughts, feelings, and surroundings in any given moment, in a gentle, non-judgmental way. In recent years, huge numbers of scientific studies have shown how a "mindfulness meditation practice" can reduce stress and enhance daily life in a myriad of ways. Meditation is the tool or exercise that produces the state of mindfulness. Meditating just means that we practice keeping our mental attention tightly focused on any object of our choice. The best-known objects for meditation are one's own breath, or a "mantra" (a specific repeated sound or phrase).

However, for thousands of years, poets, scientists, and philosophers have been using nature (including the remarkable universe of flora, fauna, mountains, oceans, and cosmos that surround us) as a meditation object with which to build mindfulness and obtain its benefits. Hence this book.

We can feel the healing power of nature every time we step outdoors, if we can be mindfully open to the moment and are willing to be truly present in the experience with body, mind, and spirit. The combination of mindfulness with nature offers a wonderful opportunity to explore a centred, calm, and joyful state of being.

Close your eyes for a moment and bring to mind how you felt the last time you recall being truly present in nature. Perhaps it was on vacation at a spectacular natural setting, viewing a

canyon carved into a wall of rock, or walking through a forest that shaded and surrounded you. Or perhaps it was simply stepping outdoors on a day when the air first felt like spring. Pausing to centre within and enjoy this recollection may bring up a sense of spaciousness, stillness, connectedness, and wellbeing that goes beyond words.

Using nature as a metaphor to deepen our understanding of how we relate to ourselves, each other, and the world, this book seeks to provide inspiration and to suggest simple actions that will help weave the power of mindfulness and of nature into daily life.

Each one of us has the opportunity to choose in each moment to be mindful and to use nature as a touchstone that will centre and support us, uplifting body, mind, and spirit.

How to Use This Book

In this small book, we explain how to use nature as a meditation practice to renew, refresh and centre yourself, anywhere and anytime.

By offering a selection of compelling quotations inspired by nature, as seen through the eyes of poets, writers, naturalists, philosophers, and scientists across the ages, we hope you will explore these with a sense of adventure and delight.

The quotations in Part I offer a selection of mindful moments and simple exercises which are quick and easy to include in your day-to-day life. Chosen to nurture an understanding of applying mindfulness to nature, as well as to deepen a sense of awe, each excerpt invites you to take a few minutes to reflect and renew. We hope you will explore these with a sense of adventure and delight.

Part II invites you to deepen your mindfulness practice through contemplating a selection of inspirational quotations to enhance your connection to nature and sense of wellbeing. We invite you to ponder them, whether outdoors in a natural setting, on waking in the morning, or before bedtime. Reflecting on these words brings the spacious and nurturing presence of nature into the moment, no matter where you are.

May this book help you welcome mindfulness, nature, and enhanced wellbeing into your life, one moment at a time.

Engaging the Mindful Breath

Before you delve into Part I, prepare yourself by engaging the mindful breath, a simple and easy exercise that will help centre you and connect you more deeply with the quotations and contemplations in in this section.

To activate the mindful breath simply focus your attention on your breathing:

1. As you inhale through your nose, follow your breath all the way down to your stomach: notice how your chest expands as your breath fills it.
2. Hold for 3 seconds, then gently and slowly exhale, allowing your breath to travel with ease up through your body and out through your mouth.
3. You might notice thoughts popping up; simply acknowledge these, without judgement, and refocus your attention on your breath.
4. Continue the mindful breathing for 3-5 minutes, or until you feel grounded and centred in the present moment.

PART I

Exploring Mindfulness in Nature:

Seeking Simplicity,

Experiencing Wonder

If we could see the miracle
of a single flower clearly, our
whole life would change.

THE BUDDHA

2,500 years ago, Siddhartha Gautama, known as the Buddha, began to develop a mental and spiritual discipline that has come to be known as mindfulness meditation. The connection between mindfulness and nature was beautifully stated when he noted how being fully present with the "miracle" of a single flower could change our understanding of the world.

Although seeing just one flower clearly is harder than it might seem, there's a simplicity at the heart of the Buddha's suggestion that makes this approachable. We don't need to take a month off to trek in the Himalayas, or hike the trail. We simply need to be willing to learn how to focus our attention and be fully present in any given moment, mindfully aware of our thoughts, feelings, and surroundings.

Opportunities to be mindful in nature abound, yet sometimes we are distracted and unable to notice or recognize such moments as they occur. As with anything we seek to learn, we need to practice this new behaviour of being mindful, and we need to make time for the small efforts that, cumulatively, have the power to change our whole life.

In this section, you'll find suggestions that invite mindfulness—and mindfulness in nature—into your life on a daily basis whether you live in the country or the town. They will take only a few minutes and you will find that this practice can fit seamlessly into your life. As you practice, let yourself experience the sense of spaciousness, wellbeing, and connection that comes when you deepen your understanding of the natural world, and enhance your connection to those who inhabit it. As you embrace this new awareness, you'll find that this shift can bring joy to your life, day by day and moment to moment.

As a single footstep will not
make a path on the earth,
so a single thought will not make a
pathway in the mind. To make
a deep physical path, we walk
again and again.
To make a deep mental path,
we must think over and over the
kind of thoughts we wish
to dominate our lives.

HENRY DAVID THOREAU

This image of walking in nature beautifully captures what science has come to understand about how the mind works. Our brains are composed of cells called neurons that link together to form neural pathways that underlie all of our actions, thoughts, and emotions. Every time we do, think, or feel something new, a neural pathway is formed. Every time that pathway is used or even remembered, more neurons join to make the neural pathway thicker and more easily "travelled." Much of a mindfulness practice involves noticing and identifying our most common neural pathways so that we can begin to choose where to place our attention. Or, choose to create new ones by starting a new practice of meditation.

Pay attention to thoughts that arise. As with favorite paths which we choose to walk repeatedly in nature, we can choose the neural pathway that we deepen by repetition in our brains. Resolve to strengthen neural pathways for actions, thoughts, and feelings that enhance your wellbeing and let go of those that create unhappiness or stress.

Everything has beauty,

but not everyone sees it.

CONFUCIUS

Even outdoors in the grandeur of nature, there may be times when we're so preoccupied with our thoughts that we're barely aware of the world around us. Becoming aware that our attention has been hijacked—often to fears, desires, or other emotions—can become the base for a practice of mindfulness that will help us learn to control our attention and avoid getting stuck in a mental fog.

Being able to notice the flowers means being able to focus on good and beautiful things in life, even when things are not going well and we are likely to be focused on negative thoughts. Being able to momentarily pay attention to, and appreciate, the beautiful and the good applies to all aspects of life.

Today be aware of the "flowers in your life" and take a moment to savour and enjoy them.

In all things of nature, there is
something marvelous.

ARISTOTLE

Nature is all around us, if we're willing to perceive it. From the sunlight we feel on our skin as we walk down a path or a busy urban street, to the raindrops that catch us unaware, to the grass growing through the cracks in a concrete sidewalk, nature offers opportunities to marvel at each moment, when we are mindfully present in the experience.

Outdoors or indoors, whether on a bustling city street or in the country, practice noticing the natural world. Pay close attention to what you perceive. Do so without judgment, without telling yourself a story about it in words. Do you see it? Hear it? Smell it? Feel it on your skin?

Whether you call this immersion "forest bathing" or "mindfulness in nature"—simply observe, carefully, with all your senses. As you do so, be in touch with the wonder of the moment. Feel your sense of connection with the natural world expand. Feel the joy that comes with this connection, no matter where you are.

The best thing one can do when it's raining is to let it rain.

HENRY WADSWORTH LONGFELLOW

In addition to rain, there are many things in life we cannot change. Nature offers us opportunities on a daily basis to explore and deepen our understanding of how a mindful approach to life can make a difference. When it rains, even if we had wanted to go out and work in the garden, we can still notice the power and beauty of the storm and appreciate the water nurturing the thirsty earth.

Mindfulness invites us to simply be present in the moment with what is, accept it for what it is, and feel compassion for our impatience, annoyance, and desire to see it be different.

When nature or life provides opportunities in which your preferences are not being met, take several slow, full breaths. Gently notice and feel each inhale and each exhale. Let go of judgmental thoughts (such as "It shouldn't be this way!" or "I hate when that happens!") and be present in the moment, appreciating the opportunity to work with mindfulness in real time.

Should you shield the canyons from the wind storms you would never see the true beauty of their carvings.

ELISABETH KÜBLER-ROSS

In nature, storms shape the canyons to create remarkable carvings. Similarly, in daily life, we have experiences that are stressful, unanticipated, painful, and out of our control. As we appreciate the beauty that comes from upheaval or disturbance in the natural world, we can recognize that it takes the rough-and-tumble of real and even painful experiences to shape us, and that these events are opportunities for growth.

Each time we practice being mindfully present in the moment and address a bad mood, a stubbed toe, or a blow to our self-esteem with equanimity, we strengthen our practice, and thus make ourselves—carve ourselves—into a slightly more skillful person.

When something unpleasant happens, notice what's going on in your body. As the annoyance occurs, your body will probably tense up. Your jaw may clench; your breathing may get shallow. As you experience this, consciously relax your muscles and turn your attention to your breath. Soften around the stress and let it go. The more often you do this, the easier it becomes.

If you look deep enough you
will see music; the heart of nature
being everywhere music.

THOMAS CARLYLE

Being outdoors in a natural setting and being mindfully aware of your senses creates an opportunity to experience the magic of all that is.

Choose a quiet place where you can go to explore "deep listening" in nature. Whether in a garden, a park, the beach, or a neighborhood street lined with trees, spend at least ten minutes simply being present in the moment.

As you breathe gently and fully, release your thoughts and focus exclusively on the sounds around you. As you listen without mental distraction, you will likely begin to hear a tapestry of sound that was previously outside your awareness. What do you hear close by? What can you hear in the distance? Delight in the music of the Earth as it washes over you.

To see a world in a grain of sand

And heaven in a wild flower

Hold infinity in the palm of your hand

And eternity in an hour.

WILLIAM BLAKE

As we continue to be mindful in nature—present in the moment, in touch with our senses, and simply aware of what is—we may begin to feel a sense of spaciousness as the mind becomes clear of thoughts. Practice being present in the moment in a natural setting that nurtures an expansiveness within you. It may be a setting with a view. It may be the tiniest part of the natural world, a single flower. Breathe gently and fully as you focus attention on it, and invite a sense of spaciousness to inform your awareness.

How might infinity feel in your mind and heart?
What might eternity feel like as it embraced
you?

Nature does not hurry.

Yet everything is accomplished.

LAO TZU

As we look to nature for guidance on how to live,
we can see that there are insights to be drawn from
the world around us. Nature has a pace all her own.
From the movement of glaciers that shaped the earliest
years of our planet to the planting of trees in the spring,
nature has a time-frame that encompasses all.

If you feel rushed and stressed, take a slow, full, mindful breath and remind yourself that there is a flow to getting things done. Become aware that rushing and multi-tasking are more often detriments to life than enhancements to it.

As you continue to breathe slowly, deeply, fully, you can align yourself with the energy of the process you've begun. As we recognize nature as our model, we understand that mindful, focused energy will help us to complete our tasks more easily than frenetic haste.

Nature never deceives us;

it is we who deceive ourselves.

JEAN-JACQUES ROUSSEAU

If we see nature clearly—with eyes that perceive the reality of each moment, a mind that is free from preconceptions and incessant self-talk, and a heart that is open to all that is— nature will never deceive us.

Acknowledging that we deceive ourselves is a profound opportunity for insight. It means acknowledging our human frailties and recognizing that we may misperceive incoming information or filter it through a protective lens, or even a negative one.

Become aware if there are times when you may be deceiving yourself. As you interact with others or spend time alone, watch the mind to see if it is creating "stories" that move beyond fact. If you become aware of such stories, you can begin to ask yourself, "is this true?" and to hold the answers gently, while allowing them to inform your subsequent thoughts and actions.

Earth laughs in flowers.

RALPH WALDO EMERSON

As we spend time in nature, we find we become more attuned to the intent of the natural world. We begin to understand the ebb and flow of sunlight, the rise and fall of the moon.

From the sparseness of winter, to the renewal of spring, to the abundance of summer flowers, to the changing colors of fall, we delight in the seasons.

As you see flowers in real life or in images, feel the joy of the Earth. Feel the lightness and laughter in each flower's natural beauty and spend a moment appreciating the wonder of the natural world.

We do not see nature

with our eyes, but with our

understandings and our hearts.

WILLIAM HAZLITT

Being mindful in nature calls upon all of our senses and then moves beyond. Through seeing and hearing, using senses of touch, smell, and taste, we find ourselves opening to the moment as we explore the physical dimensions of nature's grandeur and beauty, and then move beyond words.

Simply be present and experience how it feels to be in a natural setting without using words. Take the miracle of nature into your heart and your deepest understanding. As you quiet your mind and let nature speak directly to your soul, you nurture your deepest wellbeing.

Nature will bear the closest inspection. She invites us to lay our eye level with her smallest leaf, and take an insect view of its plain.

HENRY DAVID THOREAU

It's easy to keep our attention focused on the newest TV series, or a fast-breaking story on the Internet. But we don't build "mental muscle" by looking at things that we're used to. Instead, if we spend some time practicing Thoreau's "close attention", we can increase our power to focus our mental attention exactly where we want it, and when we want it.

We do so by honing our attentional skills on less than intrinsically attractive things, like the insect-eye view of a single leaf. Or the carefully observed and detailed process of a single breath as it enters, fills the body, and then leaves, with subtle sensations throughout.

This kind of practice helps us to avoid unhelpful thoughts, whether they are judgments, desires, fears, angers, or any other unskillful mental objects that will fill our minds, if we allow them to.

Sunshine is delicious, rain is refreshing, wind braces us up, snow is exhilarating; there is really no such thing as bad weather, only different kinds of good weather.

JOHN RUSKIN

Often without realizing it, we find ourselves running a mental commentary on people, events, and things around us. When we do become aware of this internal monologue, we may be surprised at how often it is negative. Minds are used to judging: good, bad, right, wrong. Yet, when we're being mindful, there's also the possibility of simply observing.

Watch the thoughts that run through your mind and become aware of the stream of commentary. Notice if it's negative, neutral, or positive. Starting out as simply as observing your reactions to the weather, become aware that your thoughts shape your feelings. Choose to let go of "judging thoughts" and feel your emotions lighten with this mental shift.

If you truly love nature,
you'll find beauty everywhere.

VINCENT VAN GOGH

Understanding that "beauty lies in the eyes of the beholder",
as Plato noted long ago, offers an opportunity for us to take
responsibility for becoming mindful beholders. In order to
delight in the beauty and joy of nature, and in the freshness
of each moment, we need to see with new eyes.

As you look around, observe nature as if you were seeing it for the first time. Imagine yourself to be a careful and sensitive naturalist and feel a sense of awe at your discoveries, whether a thundering storm or a bug trundling across the floor. You may also explore the possibility of observing yourself and those around you with these same loving "new eyes" and perceive instances of newly discovered beauty everywhere.

Adopt the pace of nature:

her secret is patience.

RALPH WALDO EMERSON

In this 2^{1st} century, patience is often not considered much of a virtue. We eat fast, sleep short, and commend ourselves for multi-tasking. As an antidote to this frantic pace of modern life, we can practice adopting nature's pace by slowing down, for just a minute or half a minute at a time.

While eating, observe one slow mouthful, taking 10 or 20 seconds from the instant of the sandwich or food-laden fork rising to the mouth, to the swallowing of the well-chewed food.

While walking from place to place, choose one short section of your journey—even just walking across a single room—and take two or three seconds for each step, noticing the lifting, moving, and placing of the foot.

Doing this even a few times each day will relax you and deepen your mindfulness meditation practice, even if this is all you do. This is an especially valuable exercise to do when out in nature, and you may be surprised at what you will perceive when travelling for a moment, at nature's pace.

We must all obey the great
law of change. It is the most
powerful law of nature.

EDMUND BURKE

Observing nature, we can see change happening almost before our eyes, as buds blossom into flowers or summer leaves appear to turn autumnal overnight. At other times, the pace of change is imperceptible, as when the Grand Canyon was carved across millions of years. Understanding this law of nature invites us to recognize how change also permeates our own lives. Pay attention to changes large and small, both in nature and in your own life. Becoming aware of impermanence, as it inevitably comes with change, provides us with an opportunity to be mindful in choosing our responses to the ephemeral quality of life.

You can choose to rail against this law of nature and create suffering for yourself. Or you can choose to observe the process of change in the natural world and in yourself, simply noting what is happening with interest and not adding an overlay of emotion.

To such an extent does nature
delight and abound in variety that
among her trees there is not one
plant to be found which is exactly
like another; and not only
among the plants, but among the
boughs, the leaves and the fruits,
you will not find one which is
exactly similar to another.

LEONARDO DA VINCI

This quotation reminds us that nature appears to love—or at least on some level, value—individuality and difference. To be mindful in nature is to perceive abundance laid out before us, as we delight in an infinity of unique attributes.

Be aware of trees, plants, and flowers with an appreciative eye for their differences, from the obvious to the almost imperceptible. Similarly, be aware of appreciating your own unique individuality. As with nature, each person is different. By recognizing, without judgment, the variety of nature, you can begin to learn to be more accepting of yourself and others. Should feelings of judgment arise, simply refocus your total attention onto any natural object, and that moment of judgment will pass.

Much of the time, our mental stream of self-talk involves either comparing ourselves to others, or to the impossibly high standards that our culture tells us we should hold ourselves to.

Listen to da Vinci and spend a moment, every day, appreciating your own unique individuality, blemishes, quirks, and all. Notice judging thoughts that may arise ("Yes, I'm unique, but I really need to lose weight...") and gently let them go.

When the bird and the book

disagree, believe the bird.

JOHN JAMES AUDUBON

Much of the time, our mental process involves placing more attention on what we are thinking about what we perceive, than on the perception itself. When we see an object, whether a tree or a bird, or a slug, instead of simply observing the object, we engage in self-talk about it. Perhaps we label it. "That's a pine." Perhaps we judge it. "Ohh, a Red-headed Woodpecker, how beautiful." "A slug. Disgusting. Glad I didn't step on it."

When observing natural phenomena, try—at least some of the time—to simply see the colors of the flower, the sound of the waterfall, the feeling of wet leaves under bare feet. Apply that same keen observation to your mind and body. Study yourself and your reactions as though you were a rare and beautiful creature in the forest, observed by a careful and sensitive naturalist.

Love has no season.

It comes in the night of winter,

in the midday summer sun.

It has no reason to be born.

But I have never known it

to be wasted.

Seasons change...

And so, love's form.

FRIEDA FELDMAN

Change is a constant, like it or not. From the cells that are constantly being born and dying within our bodies, to the natural flow of seasons—change occurs in each moment. Some shifts are visible to us. Others are not. Whether the ageing of our bodies or the emergence of new technologies in this increasingly complex world, whether we are happy or unhappy, eager or fearful, there's no way to put change on hold.

Nature, with its inexorable power and grace, offers a respite from tumultuous times in our lives, in the world. Here's an instant intervention you can use, if you are feeling overwhelmed.

Simply go outside and breathe. Eyes open or closed, breathe fully and slowly. Fill the lungs from the bottom up as the belly expands, then release as the belly contracts. As you feel the sensation of air entering and leaving your body, relax and enjoy the breath, clearing the mind of thoughts. Let the simplicity of nature bring clarity and depth to this moment.

As you do this for three minutes, a sense of spaciousness begins to flow with the breath, and with this spaciousness comes a choice. You can choose to bring this sense of serenity with you as you step back to the complexities of the moment. You can recognize that each moment is an opportunity to be mindfully present, whether outdoors or in.

This poem offers a reminder that, similar to nature, love—with its strength and joy—is also part of the changing world and is everywhere, if we are open to it.

PART II

Inspirational Contemplations to Further

your Practice

Introduction to Part II

Nature calls forth in us a joy that elevates ordinary moments, and a humility that offers a touchstone for understanding the Universe, as it simultaneously centres us deeply in the moment.

On the pages that follow, you will find inspirational quotations from writers, naturalists, poets, artists, and philosophers across the centuries—and even millennia—offering a tribute to the power of nature to expand our hearts and mind.

These insights, inspired by the beauty, grandeur, mystery, and simplicity of nature offers you an opportunity to deepen your mindfulness practice through the gentle yet powerful art of contemplation. Take time to pause and reflect on each excerpt noting the thoughts, feelings and sensations you experience. Consider the role that mindfulness in nature has, or might have, in the context of your own life.

For a more meaningful experience of this section, complete the following breathing exercise before reading on.

Engaging the Mindful Breath

This simple and easy breathing exercise will help centre you and connect you more deeply with the quotations that follow.

To activate the mindful breath simply focus your attention on your breathing:

1. As you inhale through your nose, follow your breath all the way down to your stomach: notice how your chest expands as your breath fills it.
2. Hold for 3 seconds, then gently and slowly exhale, allowing your breath to travel with ease up through your body and out through your mouth.
3. You might notice thoughts popping up; simply acknowledge these, without judgement, and refocus your attention on your breath.
4. Continue the mindful breathing for 3-5 minutes, or until you feel grounded and centred in the present moment.
5. This quick and effective practice can be used regularly to centre yourself, connect with Nature and renew your sense of wellbeing.

The clearest way into the Universe
is through a forest wilderness.

JOHN MUIR

There is a pleasure in the pathless woods,

There is a rapture in the lonely shore,

There is society where none intrudes,

By the deep sea, and music in its roar;

I love not Man the less, but Nature more.

LORD BYRON

Nature offers unceasingly the most novel and fascinating objects for learning.

ALEXANDER VON HUMBOLDT

To sit in the shade on a fine day,

and look upon verdure, is the most

perfect refreshment.

JANE AUSTEN

If I spent enough time with

the tiniest creature—even a

caterpillar—I would never have

to prepare a sermon.

So full of God is every creature.

MEISTER ECKHART

The subtlety of nature is greater
many times over than the subtlety
of the senses and understanding.

FRANCIS BACON

I can enjoy society in a room;
but out of doors, nature is company
enough for me.

WILLIAM HAZLITT

Heaven is under our feet as
well as over our heads.

HENRY DAVID THOREAU

My miserable hearing does
not trouble me here.
In the country it seems as if every
tree said to me: 'Holy! Holy!' Who
can give complete expression to the
ecstasy of the woods! O, the sweet
stillness of the woods!

LUDWIG VAN BEETHOVEN

To the mind that is still, the whole

universe surrenders.

LAO TZU

I loafe and invite my soul,

I lean and loafe at my ease

observing a spear of summer grass.

WALT WHITMAN

Nature is what we know—yet have

not art to say—

So impotent our wisdom is

to her simplicity.

EMILY DICKINSON

Nature understands no jesting;
she is always true, always serious,
always severe; she is always right,
and the errors and faults are
always those of man.

JOHANN WOLFGANG VON GOETHE

I wonder if the snow loves the trees and fields, that it kisses them so gently? And then it covers them up snug, you know, with a white quilt; and perhaps it says 'Go to sleep, darlings, till the summer comes again.'

LEWIS CARROLL

Among the scenes which are
deeply impressed on my mind, none
exceeded in sublimity the primeval
forests undefaced by the hand
of man.

CHARLES DARWIN

If you live according to nature,
you never will be poor; if according
to the world's caprice, you will
never be rich.

PUBLILIUS SYRUS

The lack of power to take joy
in outdoor nature is as real a
misfortune as the lack of power
to take joy in books.

THEODORE ROOSEVELT

What is a weed? A plant whose
virtues have yet to be discovered.

RALPH WALDO EMERSON

I go to nature to be soothed
and healed, and to have my
senses put in order.

JOHN BURROUGHS

A thing of beauty is a joy forever.

JOHN KEATS

And this, our life, exempt from
public haunt, finds tongues in
trees, books in the running brooks,
sermons in stones, and good
in everything.

WILLIAM SHAKESPEARE

It is not so much for its beauty
that the forest makes a claim upon
men's hearts, as for that subtle
something, that quality of air that
emanation from old trees, that so
wonderfully changes and renews
a weary spirit.

ROBERT LOUIS STEVENSON

Nature can do more

than physicians.

OLIVER CROMWELL

When one tugs at a single thing
in nature, he finds it attached to
the rest of the world.

JOHN MUIR

Summer afternoon; to me
those have always been the two
most beautiful words in the
English language.

HENRY JAMES

The tree which moves some
to tears of joy is in the eyes
of others only a green thing
that stands in the way.
Some see nature all ridicule
and deformity... and some scarce
see nature at all. But to the eyes
of the man of imagination,
nature is imagination itself.

WILLIAM BLAKE

Nature has spread for us a
rich and delightful banquet.
Shall we turn from it?

THOMAS COLE

Nature gives to every time and
season some beauties of its own.

CHARLES DICKENS

Every particular in nature,

a leaf, a drop, a crystal, a moment

of time is related to the whole,

and partakes of the perfection

of the whole.

RALPH WALDO EMERSON

Nature! We are surrounded
and embraced by her: powerless to
separate ourselves from her...

JOHANN WOLFGANG VON GOETHE

Here and elsewhere we shall not
obtain the best insight into things
until we actually see them
growing from the beginning.

ARISTOTLE

Long before I learned to do a sum in arithmetic or describe the shape of the earth, Miss Sullivan had taught me to find beauty in the fragrant woods, in every blade of grass...

HELEN KELLER

All art is but imitation of nature.

SENECA

Nature is an infinite

sphere of which the centre

is everywhere and the

circumference nowhere.

BLAISE PASCAL

There are no words that
can tell the hidden spirit of the
wilderness, that can reveal its
mystery, its melancholy,
and its charm.

THEODORE ROOSEVELT

Nature is painting for us, day after day, pictures of infinite beauty, if only we have the eyes to see them. The earth has received the embrace of the sun and we shall see the results of that love.

JOHN RUSKIN

Words, like nature, half reveal and
half conceal the soul within.

ALFRED LORD TENNYSON

Live in each season as it passes;
breathe the air, drink the drink,
taste the fruit, and resign yourself
to the influence of the earth.

HENRY DAVID THOREAU

If I were to name the three most precious resources of life, I should say books, friends, and nature; and the greatest of these, at least the most constant and always at hand, is nature.

JOHN BURROUGHS

Nature, whose sweet rains fall on unjust and just alike, will have clefts in the rocks where I may hide, and secret valleys in whose silence I may weep undisturbed.

OSCAR WILDE

To me a lush carpet of pine needles or spongy grass is more welcome than the most luxurious Persian rug.

HELEN KELLER

Let Nature be your teacher.

WILLIAM WORDSWORTH

Keep a green bough in your heart
and a singing bird will come.

LAO TZU

Let the clean air blow the cobwebs

from your body. Air is medicine.

LILLIAN RUSSELL

Those who contemplate the beauty
of the earth find reserves of
strength that will endure as
long as life lasts.
There is something infinitely healing
in the repeated refrains of nature—
the assurance that dawn comes
after night, and spring after winter.

RACHEL CARSON

All my life I have tried to pluck a thistle

and plant a flower wherever the flower

would grow in thought and mind.

ABRAHAM LINCOLN

To the artist there is never anything ugly in nature.

AUGUSTE RODIN

Even kings and emperors

with heaps of wealth and vast

dominion cannot compare

with an ant filled with the

love of God.

GURU NANAK

Flowers are the sweetest things

that God ever made and forgot to

put a soul into.

HENRY WARD BEECHER

Don't live by your own rules,

but in harmony with nature.

EPICTETUS

It is not half so important to know
as to feel when introducing a young
child to the natural world.

RACHEL CARSON

I might mention all the divine charms of a bright spring day, but if you had never in your life utterly forgotten yourself in straining your eyes after the mounting lark, or in wandering through the still lanes when the fresh-opened blossoms fill them with a sacred, silent beauty like that of fretted aisles, where would be the use of my descriptive catalogue?

GEORGE ELIOT (MARY ANNE EVANS)

Nature is always new in the spring,

and lucky are we if it finds

us new also.

JOHN BURROUGHS

Remind thyself that he whom thou lovest is mortal, that what thou lovest is not thine own; it is given thee for the present, not irrevocably nor forever, but even as a fig or a bunch of grapes at the appointed season of the year.

EPICTETUS

Nature's peace will flow into
you as sunshine flows into trees.

JOHN MUIR

Every leaf speaks bliss to me

Fluttering from the autumn tree.

EMILY BRONTË

I'd give all the wealth that years have piled,

The slow results of life's decay,

To be once more a little child

For one bright summer day.

LEWIS CARROLL

I would wish that all young persons
might be exhorted to read the
great book of nature, wherein they
may see the wisdom and power of
the Creator, in the order of the
universe, and in the production
of all things.

· ANN BAYNARD

To the lover of birds, insects,
and plants, the smallest area
around a well-chosen home will
furnish sufficient material to satisfy
all thirst of knowledge through
the longest life.

MARY TREAT

...a traveller should be a botanist,
for in all views plants form the
chief embellishment.

CHARLES DARWIN

How came the bodies of animals to be

contrived with so much art, and for

what ends were their several parts?

Was the eye contrived without skill

in Opticks, and the ear without

knowledge of sounds?

ISAAC NEWTON

Give me solitude—give me Nature—give me again, O Nature, your primal sanities!

WALT WHITMAN

Nature is a revelation of God;

Art is a revelation of man.

HENRY WADSWORTH LONGFELLOW

Climb the mountains

and get their good tidings.

Nature's peace will flow into you as

sunshine flows into trees. The winds

will blow their own freshness into

you, and the storms their energy,

while cares will drop off

like autumn leaves.

JOHN MUIR

The poetry of the earth

is never dead.

JOHN KEATS

Keep your love of nature, for that
is the true way to understand art
more and more.

VINCENT VAN GOGH

The sun shines not on us but in us.

JOHN MUIR

A man is related to all nature.

RALPH WALDO EMERSON

One touch of nature makes

the whole world kin.

WILLIAM SHAKESPEARE

In the spring, I have counted
136 different kinds of weather
inside of 24 hours.

MARK TWAIN

A Final Note

We hope that the quotes, ideas, and suggestions in this book will help you to explore the remarkable opportunities for expanded awareness and personal growth available through mindfulness in nature.

As you practice opening your mind, your heart, and your spirit to the simplicity and immediacy of both mindfulness and nature, you'll find that you begin to carry within yourself a sense of spaciousness and centredness.

Know that each time you are truly present in the moment, appreciating the natural world, you deepen and strengthen the mental pathways that connect you to this sense of wellbeing. Know that each time you recall how it feels to be present in this way, you're doing the same. Every time you do this, it becomes easier to do—more natural, as it were—as mindfulness in nature becomes "second nature" to you!

May your life be enriched by mindfulness in nature, bringing you moments of joy and memories to savour. May you also feel uplifted as you experience new ways of being present—one moment at a time.

Both David and Nina delight in being outdoors. They have found, along with many others, comfort and support for living in an increasingly complex world from the profound simplicity of being mindful in nature.

About Trigger Publishing

Trigger is a leading independent altruistic global publisher devoted to opening up conversations about mental health and wellbeing. We share uplifting and inspirational mental health stories, publish advice-driven books by highly qualified clinicians for those in recovery and produce wellbeing books that will help you to live your life with greater meaning and clarity.

Founder Adam Shaw, mental health advocate and philanthropist, established the company with leading psychologist Lauren Callaghan, whilst in recovery from serious mental health issues. Their aim was to publish books which provided advice and support to anyone suffering with mental illness by sharing uplifting and inspiring stories from real life survivors, combined with expert advice on practical recovery techniques.

Since then, Trigger has expanded to produce books on a wide range of topics surrounding mental health and wellness, as well as launching Ups!de Down Books, its children's list, which encourages open conversation around mental health from a young age.

We want to help you to not just survive but thrive... one book at a time.

Find out more about Trigger Publishing by visiting our website: triggerpublishing.com or join us on:
Twitter **@TriggerPub**
Facebook **@TriggerPub**
Instagram **@TriggerPub**

About the Shaw Mind Foundation

A proportion of profits from the sale of all Trigger books go to their sister charity, The Shaw Mind Foundation, also founded by Adam Shaw and Lauren Callaghan. The charity aims to ensure that everyone has access to mental health resources whenever they need them.

You can find out more about the work that The Shaw Mind Foundation do by visiting their website:

shawmindfoundation.org

or joining them on

Twitter @**Shaw_Mind**
Facebook @**ShawMindFoundation**
Instagram @**Shaw_Mind**